Packages of Praise for Kids

brief worship services led by children

He's Alive! • The Majesty of God • Praise His Name! • Thank You, Lord!

Skits and narrations by
Pamela Clampitt Vandewalker
and **Anita Wagoner**

Companion Products Available:

Listening Cassette 0-6330-0552-5
(available at a discount when purchased in quantities of ten or more from your Music Supplier or Genevox Music Group)

Listening CD 0-6330-0553-3

Accompaniment Cassette 0-6330-0554-1 (stereo tracks only)

Accompaniment CD 0-6330-0555-X (stereo tracks only)

Cassette Promo Pak 0-6330-0557-6

CD Promo Pak 0-6330-0558-4

A division of Genevox

Code 0-6330-0551-7

© Copyright 1999 GENEVOX (a div. of GMG), Nashville, TN 37234.

Foreword

Packages of Praise for Kids is designed to give children the opportunity to lead in worship or chapel services. It is self-contained and designed to set up a sermon or devotional thought. There are four themes contained in this collection. These are Easter, Thanksgiving, praise, and creation. Each section can be done as presented, or, if a shorter segment is desired, choose a narration introduction and a song. If a longer service is desired, pull two themes together to create a full evening or program.

Before each section there is an introduction page with performance suggestions and hints, props needed, solos, characters for the drama, and narration clues. The best thing to remember is that what is listed is only one presentation. Many of the narrations are versatile enough to use from 2 to 15 speaking roles. Adapt them to fit your needs. Be creative and include as many of the children as you can. They will enjoy being a part and will take ownership in services and ministries in the future.

God's blessings on you as you lead our future leaders.

Contents

He's Alive! 4
Lord, I Lift Your Name on High 7
Have You Heard? 12
Crown Him with Many Crowns 16

The Majesty of God 22
The Majesty of God 23
I Can Praise the Lord 30
I Sing the Mighty Power of God 36
I See God 39

Thank You, Lord! 43
Count Your Blessings 44
It Is Good to Give Thanks 51
Attitude of Gratitude 55

Praise His Name! 60
Rock of My Salvation 61
Jesus Is All the World to Me 70
There Is Power in the Wonderful Name 76
My God Is Mighty 81

He's Alive!

by Pamela Clampitt Vandewalker

Characters for Drama

(Feel free to vary this to fit your needs. For example, use 2 boys and 2 girls, etc.)

<table>
<tr><td>Tiffany</td><td>Matt</td><td>Angela</td></tr>
<tr><td>Mandy</td><td></td><td>Mom</td></tr>
</table>

Scene

Beach area *(this can be implied by the use of attire for the characters and the props used.)* The sound effects of a beach are available on the accompaniment CD.

Props

5 buckets, shells, large shell, sand dollar *(can use something like a round cracker to suggest a sand dollar shell)*

Songs

"Lord, I Lift Your Name on High" – unison choir
"Have You Heard?" – unison choir
"Crown Him with Many Crowns" – unison choir

Staging Suggestions

Choir can be in place as drama begins. They can observe the drama and stand and sing the song. Feel free to ask the congregation to join "Lord, I Lift Your Name on High" at ms. 17 the second time. The narration before "Have You Heard?" should be delivered with excitement and confidence. Depending on your use of microphones, these lines can be said by the kids from the choir.

(Scene up on children with buckets and beachwear. The children are collecting seas shells. *Sound effects of sea gulls and the surf coming in.)

TIFFANY: This is so much fun!

MANDY: I've almost gotten my bucket completely full of shells.

MATT: How'd you do that so fast?

MANDY: *(pulling out large shell)* Look at this one I found.

(Children gather around to see the shell.)

ANGELA: Neat ... that's a big one.

MANDY: *(proudly)* Yeah ... it is.

MATT: *(taking it from her and putting it to his ear)* Let's listen and see if we can hear the ocean in it.

ANGELA: I want to ...

TIFFANY: Me, too!

ALL: *(ad lib, while listening to the shell)* Cool ... Neat ... etc.

MOM: *(off-stage)* Kids ... it's time to come in ... almost time to eat ...

MATT: *(yelling back)* Mom ... come here and see the shells we collected ...

MOM: *(still off-stage)* Okay ... I'll be right there.

MANDY: *(to Angela)* What kind of shells did you get?

ANGELA: *(disappointed)* I just found a bunch of small shells.

MANDY: *(looking in bucket)* But ... they're pretty ...

ANGELA: Yeah ... I guess ...

MOM: *(entering)* What did you guys find?

MANDY: *(proudly showing)* Look at the huge one I found.

MOM: *(admiring)* Wow ...how about that.

ANGELA: And the pretty ones I found.

MOM: Beautiful.

MATT: I found this neat sea horse.

MOM: That will be nice to add to the collection. Tiffany, what did you find?

---

*Sound effects are found on the accompaniment CD at index point **15**.

TIFFANY: *(dejected)* I couldn't find anything neat ... just one little sand dollar and a few other pieces of shells.

MOM: *(excited)* Oh, a sand dollar is a very special shell.

TIFFANY: *(not understanding)* It is?

MOM: Oh, yes, it is. I guess dinner can wait for a minute. Why don't you all sit down and let me tell you all about the sand dollar.

(Children sit. Mom holds sand dollar and begins to tell story.)

MOM: See, the sand dollar tells us about the birth and death of our friend Jesus.

MATT: How?

MOM: Just listen and let me show you ... See ... here in the center is the star that appeared to the Wise Men in helping them find their way to Baby Jesus.

MANDY: Cool!

MOM: IT really is ... but look here ... there's more to the story. See the four nail holes and a fifth one made by the Roman's spear in Jesus' side?

TIFFANY: Yeah, I see it!

MOM: Those holes remind us of Jesus' sacrifice for us when He died on the cross fo our sins. *(pause)* But look ... there's also an Easter lily, the symbol of Christ's resurrection. Christ didn't stay in the tomb ... He arose and He lives. When you break the sand dollar open *(breaking it)*, see ... here are five little white doves waiting to spread peace. It's like a symbol reminding us that we need to tell others that Jesus is alive!

MANDY: That's too cool!

(Others ad lib agreement.)

ANGELA: Tiffany, it looks like you may have found the neatest shell of all!

TIFFANY: *(happily)* Yeah!!!!

MOM: Come on, let's go eat!

(Children ad lib excitement as they exit stage.)

Lord, I Lift Your Name on High

Words and Music by
RICK FOUNDS
Arranged by Dick Tunney

© Copyright 1989 Maranatha Praise, Inc. (admin. by The Copyright Company, Nashville, TN).
All rights reserved. International copyright secured. Used by permission.

CHILD 1: We do praise Jesus' name!
CHILD 2: Because He is risen, just like He said.
CHILD 3: We must tell others, He rose from the dead.
CHILD 4: It was impossible for death to keep its hold on Him.
CHILD 5: Because …
ALL: Jesus died but rose again!
(Music begins.)
CHILD 1: Have you heard?
ALL: Jesus is alive!

Based on Matthew 28:6-7; Acts 2:24; I Thess. 4:14

Have You Heard?

Words and Music by
LARRY BRYANT and LOWELL ALEXANDER
Arranged by Dick Tunney

© Copyright 1995 Sony Wonder (adm. by Sony/ATV Music Publishing), 8 Music Sq. W., Nashville, TN 37203.
All Rights Reserved. Used by Permission.

16

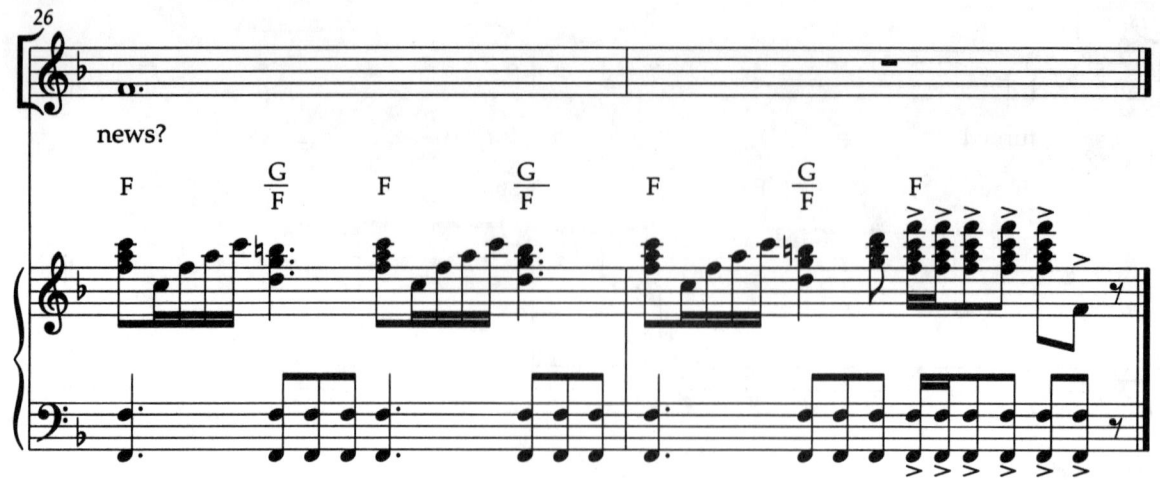

news?

Crown Him with Many Crowns

Words by
MATTHEW BRIDGES (st. 1 & 3) and
GODFREY THRING (st. 2)

Music by
GEORGE ELVEY
Arranged by John Chisum

Rhythmic (♩ = 112)
N.C.

© Copyright 1998 ThreeFold Amen Music (ASCAP) c/o ROM Administration,
8315 Twin Lakes Drive, Mobile, AL 36695. Used by Permission.

The Majesty of God

by Pamela Clampitt Vandewalker

The narration before the first song, "The Majesty of God," gives an introduction to the theme of creation. It can be done by two or three children. The choir can end the narration by joining in the last line, "Creator!"

The narration before "I Can Praise the Lord" may use as many as ten children. Just assign a different child to each line. For further participation of the choir, ask them to say the ALL lines.

For the poem before "I Sing the Mighty Power of God," you may use as many as 14 different speakers or as few as one. However many do it, practice so the rhyming is smooth and free-flowing. After the line about "broccolli, cabbage, and even beets," be sure to pause long enough for some audience laughter.

The last narration ties the idea of God's creation giving us a reason to celebrate. The lines can be delivered by two to five children. If you wish, add the choir on the word "celebrate."

Songs

"The Majesty of God" – two-part choir with opt. solo on verse 2
"I Can Praise the Lord" – unison with opt. two-part choir
"I Sing the Mighty Power of God" – unison with opt. two-part choir
"I See God" – unison with four opt. solos

CHILD 1: We are here tonight to praise the Maker of the Universe!

CHILD 2: The Lord is the everlasting God … the Creator of the ends of the earth.

CHILD 3: The universe was formed at His command.

CHILD 1: Tonight, we celebrate His mighty work!

(Music begins.)

CHILD 2: We give praise to Him for creating this vast, wonderful, and awesome world!

CHILD 3: We give Him all the glory …

CHILD 1: For He alone is our …

ALL: Creator!

The Majesty of God

Words and Music by
JANET McMAHAN-WILSON and TED WILSON
Arranged by Barny Robertson

First time - CHOIR
Second time - SOLO mp

1. I hear His voice ___ in the sounds of the earth, His pow-ers re-vealed ___ in the
2. I trust His truth, ___ I be-lieve He cares, I know ___ He an-swers ___

© Copyright 1988 BMG Songs, Inc. (ASCAP) and Careers-BMG Music Publishing, Inc. (BMI)/
Little Lion Music and Lion One Music (divs. of Bridgestone MultiMedia Group).
All rights reserved. Used by permission.

CHILD 1: The heavens declare the majesty of God!
CHILD 2: The stars proclaim the work of His hands!
CHILD 3: The Lord made the heavens, the earth, the sea,
CHILD 4: And all that is in them!
CHILD 1: Everything God made shows His glory …
CHILD 2: The beasts of the field
CHILD 3: The birds of the heavens
CHILD 4: And the fish of the sea.
ALL: He is worthy …
CHILD 1: Because …

(Music begins.)

CHILD 2: He created
ALL: All things!

Based on Psalm 19:1; Psalm 8:7-8; Rev. 4:11

I Can Praise the Lord

Words and Music by
JOANNE and MILTON LeDOUX
Arranged by Don Marsh

© Copyright 1996 Van Ness Press, Inc. (ASCAP).
Distributed by DOVETAIL MUSIC (a div. of GMG), Nashville, TN 37234.

CHILD 1: God made every living thing!
CHILD 2: Things that crawl and things with wings.
CHILD 3: He made the light that sparkles on the snow,
CHILD 4: And the soft breeze that gently blows.
CHILD 5: He's the Maker of majestic snowcapped peaks,
CHILD 6: And tiny little things that go "squeak."
CHILD 7: With His hand He calms the waves;
CHILD 8: He makes cats, gnats, and bats in caves.
CHILD 9: He creates everything we eat.

CHILD 10: *(complaining)* Like broccolli, cabbage, and even beets!
CHILD 11: Only God can make a rainbow and sunrise.
CHILD 1: Because He alone is powerful, awesome, and wise.
CHILD 2: Everywhere you look you see His touch.
CHILD 3: Showing us He loves us so very, very much!

I Sing the Mighty Power of God

Words by
ISAAC WATTS

Traditional English melody
Arranged by Don Marsh

rise, That spread the flow-ing seas a-broad, And
known; And clouds a-rise and tem-pests blow, By

built the loft-y skies. I sing the wis-dom
or-der from Thy throne; While all that bor-rows

that or-dained The sun to rule the day; The
life from Thee Is ev-er in Thy care, And

moon shines full at His com-mand, And all the stars o-
ev-'ry-where that man can be, Thou, God, are pres-ent

22
rit.
f
a tempo
bey. there. While all that bor - rows
Gsus G G Eb Ebsus/F Eb/G Ab Eb/G Ab Db
rit.
f a tempo
25
unis.
life from Thee is ev - er in Thy care, And
Eb Ebsus/F Eb/G Ebsus/F Eb/G Ab Eb/Ab Ab/Db Bbm7 Ebsus Eb
28
(opt. div.)
ev - 'ry - where that man can be, Thou, God, art
Dm7(b5) Eb/Db Cm7 Bbm7 Ab2 Gb6,9 Eb/F F7(b9) Bbm7 Cm7 Dbmaj7
31
pres - ent there. I sing the pow'r!
N.C. Db/Eb Eb Eb/Ab Ab Eb Ab Eb Gb Eb Ab

CHILD 1: We delight in all your creations, God.

CHILD 2: Thank You for this beautiful and wondrous world we live in.

CHILD 3: And we praise You for sending Your Son to this world to die on the cross for our sin.

CHILD 4: You are truly the Master Designer and Creator.

CHILD 5: We love You and praise You, for You give us reason each day to …

ALL: Celebrate!

I See God

Words and Music by
DAVID HAMPTON
Arranged by John M. DeVries

With excitement (♩ = 112)

I see God; He's ev-'ry-where, His love we share. Yes, I see God, whose work is on dis-play.

© Copyright 1996 Van Ness Press, Inc. (ASCAP).
Distributed by DOVETAIL MUSIC (a div. of GMG), Nashville, TN 37234.

I see God; His work I see, He lives in me. Yes,
I see God in new ways ev'ry day.
{1.
2. He's

Who paints the rainbows? Who builds mountains high? Who
here in my laughter, He's here when I'm sad. He

sends the rivers rolling on their
wants to make my heart His home to

41

I see __ God, whose work is on dis - play. __

I see __ God; __ His work I see, __ He lives in me. Yes,

I see __ God in new ways ev - 'ry

day.

Thank You, Lord!

by Pamela Clampitt Vandewalker

The first narration is a great introduction into the theme of thankfulness. This would be better conveyed if you used as many as 15 different speakers. However, one or two can pull it off richly. Move right into the song "Count Your Blessings."

The second narration can be done by eight different speakers. Just give a different line to each child and have the choir join in on the last line, "It is good to give thanks unto the Lord."

The last narration works best with five different speakers but can be done with as few as two.

Songs

"Count Your Blessings" – unison choir with opt. solo
"It Is Good to Give Thanks" – unison choir with solos
"Attitude of Grattitude" – unison choir with solo

CHILD 1:	There are so many things to be thankful for … I bet we can't count them all!
CHILD 2:	I'm thankful for trees that grow so very tall.
CHILD 3:	For football,
CHILD 4:	Basketball,
CHILD 5, 6, & 7:	And the *Mall!*
CHILD 6:	I like colors of all different hues, like yellow,
CHILD 7:	Reds,
CHILD 8:	And pretty shades of blue.
CHILD 9:	God gives us our teachers,
CHILD 10:	Friends,
CHILD 11:	Moms and Dads
CHILD 12:	Even e-mail … that's totally rad!
CHILD 13:	I'm thankful for zebras with stripes.
CHILD 14:	And watermelons that are really ripe!
CHILD 15:	It's like God gives us each a treasure chest full of so many things you just can't keep score, because He keeps giving more and more!

Count Your Blessings

Words and Music by
PAMELA VANDEWALKER and RHONDA BARNETT
Arranged by Dick Tunney

Driving (♩ = ca. 126)

Count 'em!

Count 'em!

© Copyright 1999 Broadman Press (SESAC).
Distributed by DOVETAIL MUSIC (a div. of GMG), Nashville, TN 37234.

*"Count Your Blessings," Words and music by JOHSON OATMAN, JR. and EDWIN O. EXCELL.
Arrangement © copyright 1999 Broadman Press (SESAC).

46

CHOIR
31
live in a coun - try that is free. Oh, God's done so much for
Dsus/A D/F# Gsus G/B G7 C G
34
me. Yes, God's done so much for me. Of
C F/G G C G C Ab7
37
all of the things that God has done, The best thing He did _ was
Db Ebm Ab7 Ebm Ab7
40
send His Son. He died and rose, the vic - t'ry won. Now,
Db Db/F Gb Db/F Ebm Db

48

our thanks to Him has just be-gun. Oh, God's done so much for me. Yes, God's done so much for me. Count 'em! Count 'em! Count 'em! Count 'em! Count your bless-ings!

Count your bless-ings, name them one by one.

Count your bless-ings, see what God has done.

Count your bless-ings, name them one by one.

Count your man-y bless-ings, see what God has

done. Count your bless-ings, Name them one by one, two, three, four, five, six, sev-en, eight! Count your man-y bless-ings, see what God has done.

CHILD 1: Over a hundred and thirty times in the scripture are we told to "give thanks."

CHILD 2: Jesus was a great example of a thanks giver. Remember when He fed the 5000 people? Before He performed that miracle, Matthew says, "He … took the fives loaves and two fishes and looked into heaven and gave thanks."

CHILD 3: When Jesus raised His good friend Lazarus from the dead, the Bible says Jesus prayed to His Father and said, "I thank Thee that Thou hast heard me."

CHILD 1: You remember at the last supper, Jesus took the bread and "gave thanks."

CHILD 3: Psalm 95:2 says, "Come before His presence with thanksgiving."

CHILD 2: "Enter His gates with thanksgiving and His courts with praise, be thankful unto Him!"

CHILD 3: "In everything by prayer with thanksgiving, make your requests known to God."

CHILD 1: I Thessalonians 5:18 says, "In everything give thanks" because …

(Music begins.)

ALL: "It is a good thing to give thanks unto the Lord."

It Is Good to Give Thanks

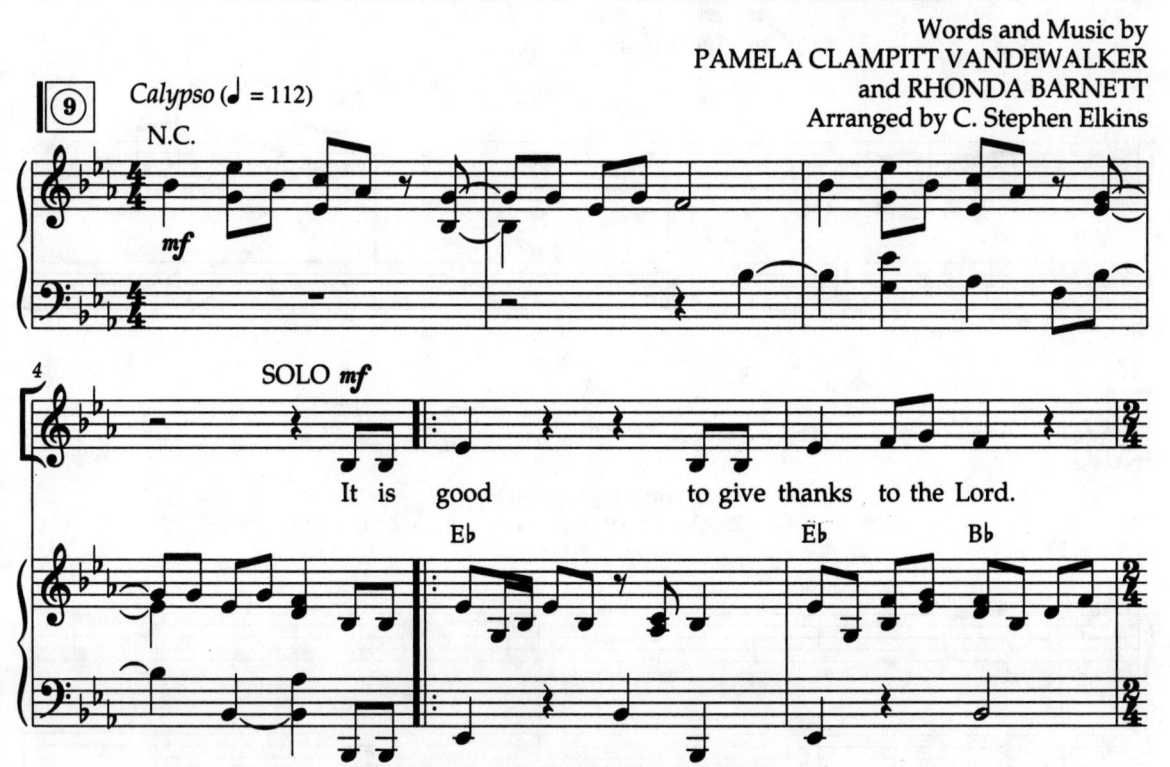

Words and Music by
PAMELA CLAMPITT VANDEWALKER
and RHONDA BARNETT
Arranged by C. Stephen Elkins

© Copyright 1997 Broadman Press (SESAC).
Distributed by DOVETAIL MUSIC (a div. of GMG), Nashville, TN 37234.

It is good to give thanks to the Lord. Ev-'ry day, ev-'ry hour, e-ven when things go so-ur. It is good to give thanks to the Lord.

1. When they pick on you at school,
2. When you see a brand new day

CHOIR **SOLO**

Give thanks! When they think you're not so cool,
Give thanks! And when things are A.-O.-K.

CHOIR **SOLO**

Give thanks! When the grade on your test gives a
Give thanks! When your mom gives a hug and you

CHOIR

pain in your chest, Give thanks, give thanks,
know you are loved,

1. give thanks! It is
2. give thanks! It is

54

CHILD 1: Even though I don't understand everything about thanksgiving, I do know it makes you feel good when someone says "thanks" to you.

CHILD 2: I remember when an old man was crossing the street and his hat blew off. I chased after it and gave it back to him. He thanked me for my help.

CHILD 3: When I say thank you, other people know I care.

CHILD 4: Last week my mom took me to the store and told me I could buy one thing. You'll never guess what kind of a store it was. It was a *kite store.* I picked out the neatest and best kite there was and then went right home and flew it high in the sky. When my mom called me in for dinner, I thanked her for the great present. And then, when I prayed to God, I told Him I was glad for the wind. I think they both know I care about them.

CHILD 5: I'm thankful Jesus is my Lord. *(Music begins.)* He is the greatest gift ever given and I want to tell others about Him. When I am thankful, others see Jesus living in me.

Attitude of Gratitude

Words by
KATHIE HILL

Music by
BILL GEORGE

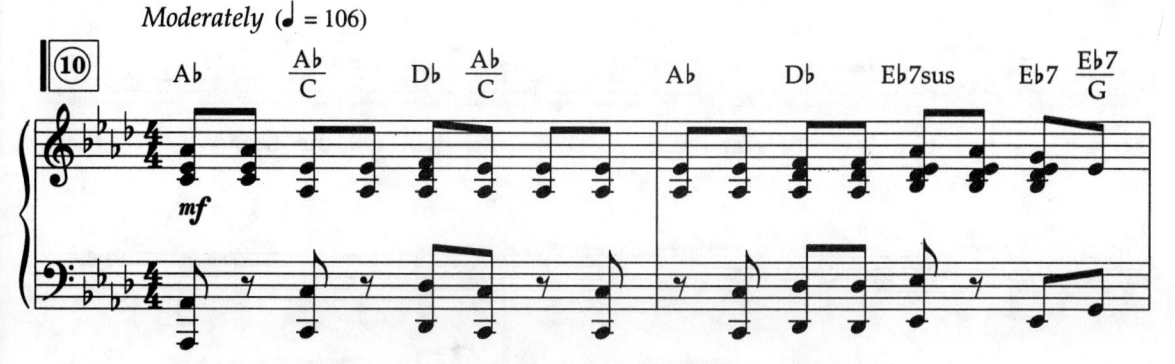

Words © copyright 1996 Van Ness Press, Inc. (ASCAP).
Distributed by DOVETAIL MUSIC (a div. of GMG), Nashville, TN 37234.
Music © copyright 1985 Ariose Music (ASCAP).
All Rights Reserved. International Copyright Secured. Used by permission.

56

CHOIR *mf*

Let's have an at-ti-tude of grat-i-tude, let's fill our hearts with praise. "Thank You, Lord," we'll say to what-ev-er comes our way. And with our at-ti-tude of grat-i-tude, our lives will tell our friends that some-thing spe - cial hap - pens when Je - sus lives with -

Third time to Coda

CHOIR - *First time*
SOLO - *Second time*

in.   1. Just im -
                                       2. ————

ag - ine what would hap - pen if you nev - er frowned,
Life's too short to spend it be - ing sad or de - pressed, In

Peo - ple all a - round would be ask - ing a - bout you.
case you have - n't guessed, God ___ wants you to be hap - py,

That's when you could tell of Je-sus' love and grace, That's
That's why we should praise Him in the good and bad. 'Cause

He's the one who placed that big smile on your face.
e-ven when you're sad, There's rea-son to be glad.
CHOIR *D.S.*
Let's have an
D.S.

CODA
in. Let's have an at-ti-tude of grat-i-tude let's

fill our hearts with praise, "Thank You, Lord," we'll say to what-ev - er comes our way. And with our at - ti - tude of grat - i - tude, Our lives will tell our friends that some - thing spe - cial hap - pens when Je - sus lives with - in. When Je - sus lives with - in!

Praise His Name!

by Anita Wagoner

Scripture reading can be read by three children. Congregation may join in reciting Psalm 72:17.

Characters

Mike
Jake
Mrs. Jessup with newborn baby

Props

baby present

possibly a bat, ball, and glove, or other sports equipment

Songs

"Rock of My Salvation" – unison choir *(congregation may join at ms. 70)*
"Jesus Is All the World to Me" – unison choir with solo
"There Is Power in the Wonderful Name" – unison choir *(congregation may join at ms. 23)*
"My God Is Mighty" – unison choir with opt. group 2 descant and opt. three-part choir

---

(Have Child 1, 2, & 3 frozen until time for them to read. Have them look up with Bible open in hand and say verse when it is their turn and then look back down at Scripture. Be very dramatic. Spotlight the children when they read if possible. Have choral group recite Psalm 72:17 with conviction.)

CHILD 1: Salvation is found in no one else, for there is no other name under heaven given to men by which we must be saved. *Acts 4:12*

GROUP: May His name endure forever ... *Psalm 72:17*

CHILD 2: Everyone who calls on the name of the Lord will be saved. *Romans 10:13*

GROUP: May His name endure forever ... *Psalm 72:17*

CHILD 3: Glorify the Lord with me; let us exalt His name forever. *Psalm 34:3*

GROUP: May His name endure forever ... *Psalm 72:17*

Rock of My Salvation

Words and Music by
SCOTT WESLEY BROWN
and DAVID HAMPTON
Arranged by Barny Robertson

Brightly (♩ = 108)

CHOIR *mf*

You are the
Rock of my __ sal - va - tion, You are the

© Copyright 1996 Songward Music (adm. The Copyright Company) and Van Ness Press, Inc. (ASCAP).
All rights reserved. Used by permission.

strength in whom I stand. You are the Rock of my salvation, You hold the righteous in Your hand. You are the Sweet-er than the hon-ey-comb,

19
Far more precious than gold,
F
Bb
F
22
is ev - 'ry word that's from You,
C
F/C
C
F/C
F/C
C
24
is ev - 'ry word that's from You.
C
F/C
C
F/C
F/C
C
26
Joy to my heart, O Lord,
Ra - diant light to my eyes.
Bb
F
Bb
F

29
Trust - wor - thy and true, Your Word is
(F) C F/C F2/C Gsus
32
trust - wor - thy and true. You are the Rock of my sal - va -
C F/C F2/C Gsus C Csus C
35
tion, You are the strength in whom I stand.
G Am C Csus C
37
You are the Rock of my sal - va - tion, You hold the
B♭ C Csus C G Am

righ - teous in __ Your hand. __

You are the Rock of my __ sal - va - tion, You are the strength in whom __ I stand. __

You are the Rock of my salvation, You hold the righteous in Your hand. Sweet-er than the hon-ey-comb, far more pre-cious than gold,

is ev-'ry word that's from You, is ev-'ry word that's from You. Joy to my heart, O Lord, Ra-diant light to my eyes, Trust-wor-thy and true, Your Word is trust-wor-thy and true. You are the Rock of my sal - va - tion, You are the strength in whom I stand, You are the Rock of my sal - va - tion, You hold the righ - teous in Your hand.

77
1
2
You are the
You hold the
D
righ - teous in Your hand.
You are the
79
D/G
A7
C2
81
Rock of my sal - va - tion!
D/F♯
G
A7
D
Dsus
D
83
You are the strength in whom I stand!
A
Bm
D/G
C/F
A7
D

Jesus Is All the World to Me

Words and Music by
WILL L. THOMPSON
Arranged by Randy Smith

I ___ would fall; When I am sad, to
I am His own. ___ He sends the sun - shine

Him I go, No oth - er one can cheer me
and the rain, He sends the har - vest's gold - en

so; When I am sad, He makes me
grain; Sun - shine and rain, Har - vest of

glad; He's my friend. ___
grain; He's my

friend.

3. Je - sus is all the world to me, and true to Him I'll be; Oh, how could I this friend de - ny, When

59
He's so true __ to me? __ Fol - low - ing
Bb13 Ab/Bb Bb/D Eb7 Eb7(b9) Abmaj7
64
Him I know I'm right, He watch-es o'er me day and
Db/Ab Eb/Ab Db2/Ab Abmaj7 Bbm7 Cm7 Bdim
70
night; Fol - low - ing Him by day and
Eb7/Bb Fm7 Gb13 Ab
3
74
night, He's my friend. __
F7(b9) Bbm7 Eb9 Ab Abmaj7

Jesus is all the world to me; He's my friend. Jesus is my friend.

JAKE:	Hey, Mike, let's go down to the park, nice day to play catch.
MIKE:	Sure thing. I just have to drop off this baby present to Mrs. Jessup for my mom. Oh, here she is now. Hi, Mrs. Jessup. *(Mrs. Jessup approaches with new baby.)*
JAKE:	Wow! That's a new baby! What's its name?
MRS. JESSUP:	Well, *it* is a little girl, and we named her Hannah, which means full of grace, because we want her always to know she is full of God's grace and our love.
MIKE:	That's neat, Mrs. Jessup. My parents named me Michael because it has something to do with being like the Lord.
MRS. JESSUP:	Well, that's a great name. I better go, guys. She gets fussy if I don't keep walking her. *(She exits.)*
JAKE:	What's the big deal with a name, anyway? That's dumb.
MIKE:	Well, when you bought your new basketball shoes, did your buy the ones the coach recommended?
JAKE:	Sure did. I got the brand name; ones with ankle support, and cushioned soles. You know, the ones that look like the pros.
MIKE:	So, the name was important, huh?
JAKE:	Yeah, guess you were right about some names. But some names can change meaning today. I mean brands and names that were popular last year may not be today.
MIKE:	That's true, but I know one name that will always retain its power and never lose its meaning.
JAKE:	What name is that?
MIKE:	The name of Jesus. He has the same power today He has always had. The Bible says that one day every knee shall bow and every tongue will confess that Jesus is Lord.
JAKE:	Yeah, that's some name.
MIKE:	Jake, remember when you went to church with me and prayed to receive Christ as Savior? The pastor said the name of Jesus is the only one with the power to save you from your sin.

JAKE: I remember. Guess some names are important, huh? But I'm still glad my parents didn't know about the meaning of baby names. They would have probably named me something that meant sweet and cute.

MIKE: No way!

(Guys exit teasing one another.)

There Is Power in the Wonderful Name

Words and Music by
ARNOLD MANKE
Arranged by Dick Tunney

1. There is pow-er in the name of Je-sus! There is
(2. There is) glo-ry in the name of Je-sus! There is

© Copyright 1984 New Spring Publishing, Inc./ASCAP, a div. of Brentwood-Benson Music Publishing, Inc.
All Rights Reserved. Unauthorized duplication prohibited.

pow-er in the name of Je - sus! There is pow-er in the
glo-ry in the name of Je - sus! There is glo-ry in the

name of Je - sus! There is pow-er in that won-der-ful name.
name of Je - sus! There is glo-ry in that won-der-ful name.

2. There is

There is heal-ing in the name of Je-sus! There is heal-ing in the name of Je-sus! There is heal-ing in the name of Je-sus! There is heal-ing in that won-der-ful name.

79

Optional Child Testimony: "What Jesus Means to Me"

(Help a child formulate four or five sentences about how Jesus has been their strength, their best friend, or a comfort to them. Rehearse their testimony but let it be genuine and personal to them.)

My God Is Mighty

Words and Music by
DAVID HAMPTON and DENNIS KURTILLA
Arranged by Don Schlosser

Driving (♩ = 120)

CHOIR *mf*

My God is might-y, ___ and He is walk-ing ___ with me; I get my strength from the Lord my God. ___ My God is might-y, ___ and He is

© Copyright 1996 Van Ness Press, Inc. (ASCAP).
Distributed by DOVETAIL MUSIC (a div. of GMG), Nashville, TN 37234.

walk - ing with me; I get my strength from the Lord my God.
Gm Dm7 Gm Cm7 D7(♯5)
Pow - er and strength are
Gm Dm7 Gm Eb2 Bb/D
His to share; There is - n't a bur - den
Cm F/A Bb Bb/D Eb2 Bb/D
He can't bear. My God is
Cm D N.C. Gm Dm7 Gm

He is — the might-y One; I get my strength from Him, And He's walk-ing with — me. He is — the might-y One; I get my strength from Him, And He's walk-ing with — me. Pow - er and strength are His to share; — There —

29
GROUP 1 f
is - n't a bur - den He can't bear.
My God is
E♭2
B♭/D
Cm D
N.C.
f
32
might - y,
and He is walk - ing with me; I get my
GROUP 2
f
He is the Might - y One; I get my strength from Him;
Gm Dm7 Gm Gm Dm7 Gm
34
strength from the Lord my God.
My God is
And He's walk - ing with me.
Cm7 D7(♯5) Gm Dm7 Gm

might-y, ___ and He is walk-ing ___ with me; I get my

He is ___ the Might-y One; I get my strength from Him,

strength from the Lord my God. ___

And He's walk-ing with ___ me.

CHOIR *f* FINGER SNAPS

My God is might-y, ___ and He is

walking with me; I get my strength from the Lord, my God.

HAND CLAPS

My God is mighty, and He is walking with me; I get my

strength from the Lord my God. I get my strength from the

Lord, my God. Lord, my God!